GLOWING ANIMALS

CONTENTS

GLORIOUS GLOWERS

Did you know that some animals glow? Some shine under certain lights, some have gleaming feathers or glow-in-the-dark skin, and others simply make light all by themselves. Welcome to the world of these glorious glowers!

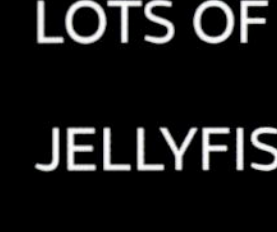

There are many ways to glow and lots of big words for different types of glowing: **LUMINESCENT**, **FLUORESCENT**, **INCANDESCENT** and even **PHOSPHORESCENT** and **BIOLUMINESCENT**. Phew, that's a lot of long words!

BIOLUMINESCENCE

Jellyfish shine using bioluminescence. No outside light or energy is needed. Instead, chemical reactions going on inside the critter create the light. Incredible, right?

Fluorescence and phosphorescence are when light is absorbed from another source. Do you have glow-in-the-dark toys? They're phosphorescent! You charge them up by putting them under a light, and they keep glowing even after the light is turned off.

ORCHID BEE

Some animals are **IRIDESCENT** and shine with a rainbow gleam, such as the one you see in a bubble. An orchid bee's metallic shine isn't made by internal heat or light. Its 'sheen' occurs as light waves bend around the insect's hard, shiny shell.

'Sea sparkle', which lights up the waves, glows with bioluminescent *Noctiluca scintillans* plankton that make their own bright blue light.

HOT OR NOT?

What's the difference between luminescence and incandescence? Turn on a lamp in your house and hold your hand near it, but don't touch it. Does your hand feel warm or stay cold? Lights that get hot are incandescent, but lights that stay cold are luminescent. Fluorescence is a kind of luminescence that needs a source of energy. When you flick the light switch off, fluorescent lights go dark right away.

THE WORLD

Before we can understand why things glow, we need to know how light works. You see, waves aren't just found at the beach – they're all around us, carrying information. Light, sound and colour all move in waves.

Soundwaves are the reason you can hear songs over the radio. Some scientists think everything in existence is actually a type of wave!

Waves go up and they come down again, taking a certain amount of time or distance to complete a cycle. Each cycle is known as a **WAVELENGTH**, a measure of the wave's frequency.

IN WAVES

COLOUR FREQUENCIES ARE TYPES OF WAVES

SOUNDS COOL?

Soundwaves of different frequencies create sounds of different pitch. Your dad's voice is probably lower than yours because the soundwaves that he's sending have a longer frequency than the ones you send back to him when you speak. High-pitched sounds, like sharp whistles or soprano singing, have higher frequencies than low-pitched sounds.

LIFE IN COLOUR

Colours have wavelengths too! Humans can only hear sounds at some frequencies, and we can only see part of the colour spectrum (the range of colours). Ultraviolet, or UV, light helps plants grow, but it has a very short wavelength and burns our skin. We can't see it, but insects and birds can, so they see light that is invisible to our eyes.

A BROWN BUTTERFLY LOOKS PURPLE UNDER UV LIGHT

SOUNDWAVES

WATT'S THE DEAL?

If colours are waves and animals glow … why? Scientists don't always know exactly why, but we can be sure there is a reason. Glowing has a *function*, or it wouldn't have evolved so many times in so many ways.

Biologists do know that glowing is a way to send messages from animals that glow (senders) to those that respond (receivers). These may be the same or different species, and the signals aren't always friendly.

Systellaspis SHRIMP

A BABY ANGLERFISH LOOKS PRETTY CUTE

Some messages lead prey into fearsome places. An anglerfish lures prey and attracts mates to a shiny light that dangles from its head. This luminescence is made by microscopic bacteria living in the anglerfish's lure. An anglerfish can also eat a meal that weighs more than it does!

Imagine swimming up to a tasty snack, only to find yourself blinded by a frightening flash! In the abyss of an ocean, where there's no light except glowing creatures, some shrimps spit glowing goo into their predators' faces.

Lanternfish in the Myctophidae family are among the most common fish in the deep oceans. Lanternfish make their own light, using chemicals called luciferins.

LET THERE BE LIGHT!

There are many ways to make light, but one of the most common involves luciferin. Does that word sound familiar? In Latin, *lucifer* means 'light-bringer' or 'bearer of light'.

Luciferin includes smaller parts (called molecules) that contain the enzyme **LUCIFERASE** and the gas oxygen, which is basically the air you breathe! When these molecules meet, they interact to create light.

LUCIFERINS

There are many types of luciferin. Researchers aren't sure whether these substances are all related to each other, but they work in similar ways. The most common luciferin found in sea life is called coelenterazine because it is used by animals in the phylum Coelenterata. See-through sea jellies (cnidarians) and sea combs (ctenophores) are collectively known as 'coelenterates'.

Lucifer is also an old name for Venus, the Morning Star. Venus was sometimes also called Phosphorus (a glowing chemical used to make matches), so you can see that the connections between ancient languages, starry skies and scientific words go back a long way.

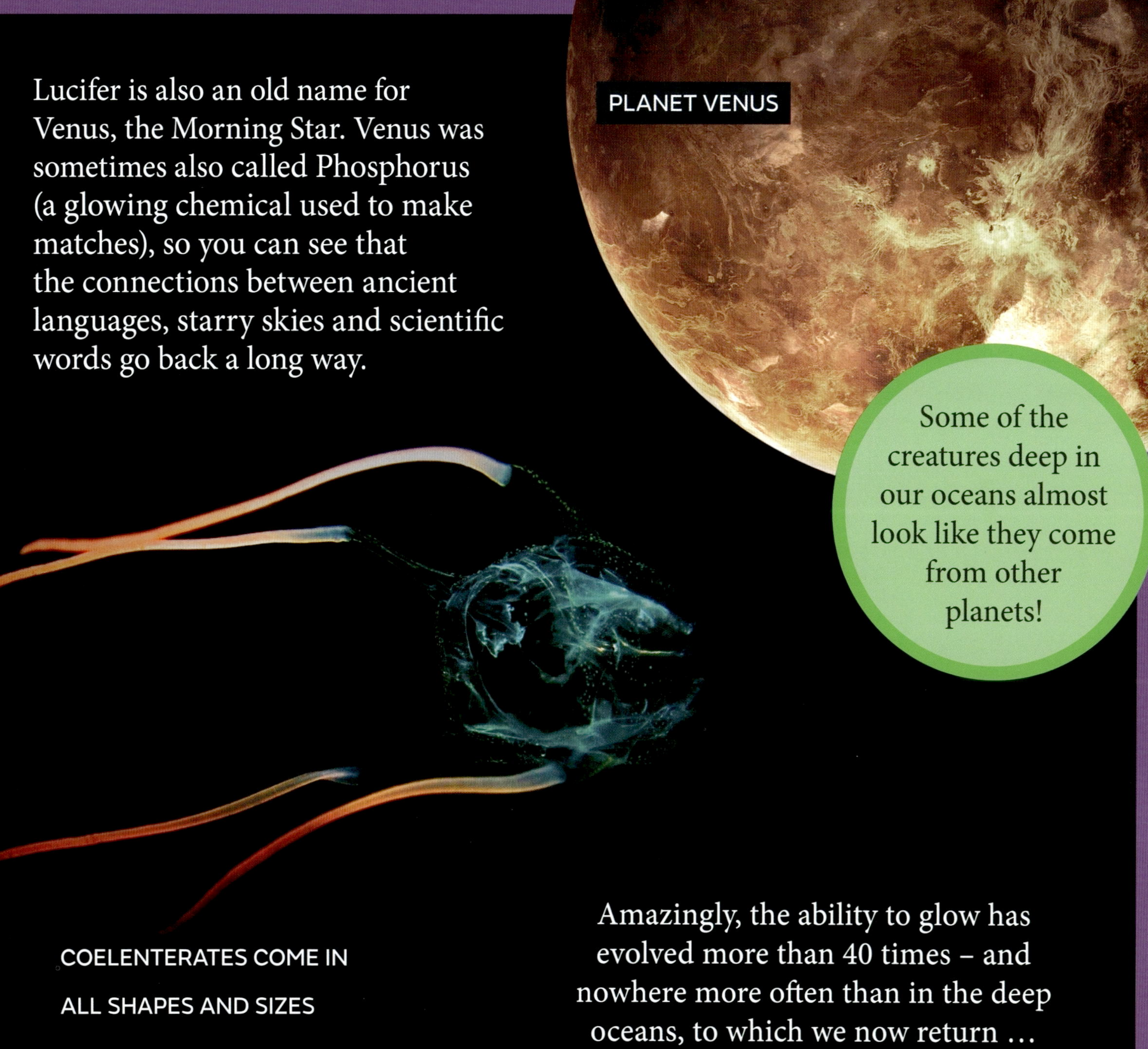

PLANET VENUS

Some of the creatures deep in our oceans almost look like they come from other planets!

COELENTERATES COME IN ALL SHAPES AND SIZES

Amazingly, the ability to glow has evolved more than 40 times – and nowhere more often than in the deep oceans, to which we now return …

SO SHINY!

Shrimps are some of the globe's best glowers. Some species have not one but two ways to glow! Glowing is such a big part of their lives that it may be involved in more than one use.

Peacock mantis shrimp have the best vision on Earth! Their compound eyes are made up of lots of tiny 'eyes' that see UV and polarised light. They can even move each eye in a different direction. Who knows what they see when they look at each other!

We've already talked about how some shrimps make gleaming goo they rudely spit at predators. Their glowing saliva is all about dazing their enemies, but many of these crustaceans also have special **PHOTOPHORES** on the sides of their bodies – and these structures have another use.

PEACOCK MANTIS SHRIMP

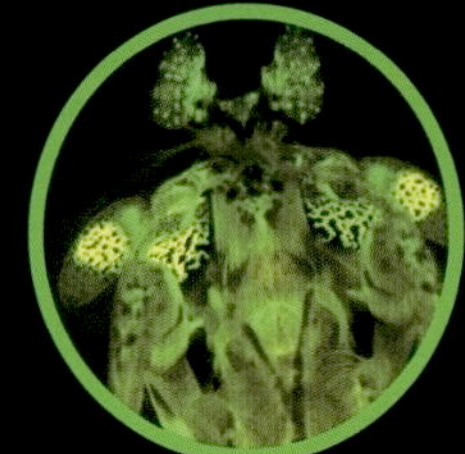

CARIBBEAN STRIPED MANTIS SHRIMP

A MANTIS SHRIMP AT DEPTH

SIGNS SENT BY LIGHT

Not all glowing shrimp have photophores, so what are they for? A clue comes from these shrimps' eyesight. Species that have photophores can see different colours to those that don't – the same colours the photophores send out. These shrimp may see fluorescent markings deep under water. Photophores may help shrimp find their own kind, or they may be like neon signs, sending signals we don't yet understand.

DID YOU KNOW?

In Greek, *photo* means 'light'. Just as the word *photograph* means 'a graph (drawing) made with light', *photophore* means 'an organ that gives off or bears light'.

ANTARCTIC KRILL

DINNER TO 'GLOW'

Tiny krill are food for much larger marine species, including enormous sperm whales. Krill can swim down to 2000m and have glow-in-the-dark organs. Sometimes, the white markings around the mouth of a sperm whale glow because it has 'chowed down' on lots of bioluminescent krill.

Scientists have photographed Caribbean striped mantis shrimps under black lights to reveal what they might look like to other mantis shrimps in the depths. What a difference the light makes!

SPERM WHALE

BUBBLE-TIP ANEMONES

GLOW BUDDIES

Creatures send signals in all sorts of ways. Sometimes an animal sending a light signal isn't making the light itself. Often, the 'light-bringer' isn't even an animal!

When two species need each other so they can survive, it is called **SYMBIOSIS**, which means 'living together'. Sometimes, one critter lives inside the other, and they're so close that it looks like they're the same animal. Bioluminescence often comes from these tiny critters (which are usually bacteria or algae) living inside other animals and making the light the larger organism uses to send its signals. This special relationship is called **ENDOSYMBIOSIS**.

Bubble-tip anemones and many corals have tiny organisms called zooxanthellae living inside them and making nutritious food for them. These little 'dinoflagellates', as they are also called, sometimes help the critter glow.

The 5-cm-long bobtail squid is cute as a button … unless you're a shrimp on its menu! It uses bioluminescence to camouflage itself, but it doesn't make its own light – bacteria on its skin do that instead.

BOBTAIL SQUID

BACTERIA BESTIES

Baby squid aren't born with their glowing bacteria best friends. As soon as they swim out into the world, bacteria find them. These bacteria use a special chemical to signal to the squid's cells that they're friendly.

Under the water, most light comes from above. Glowing bacteria on the underside of a bobtail squid create a kind of camouflage known as 'counterillumination', which hides an animal's silhouette by matching the colour of light from above.

How the bacteria find and enter squid or anglerfish isn't totally understood. Scientists also aren't exactly sure how the relationship helps the bacteria.

SLUGGISH AT THE

You might think snails and slugs are slow, but some can be said to move at the speed of light – because they're bioluminescent, too!

Nudibranchs (a funny name that just means 'naked gills') probably use their glow to startle their enemies or to warn them that these 'slugs' are toxic and deadly to eat.

Nudibranchs are slow-moving marine sea slugs – kind of like snails without shells. They are often very brightly coloured and poisonous. Some blend in with their coral surroundings until they're forced to stand out to scare off attackers. If they're at risk, special organs in the skin of some species flash with sudden light.

TILE'S SEA SLUG IN THE DARK

THE BIOLUMINESCENT TILE'S SEA SLUG IN THE LIGHT

SPEED OF LIGHT

The bearded fireworm may look a bit like a nudibranch, but it is actually a type of marine flatworm that lives in the Atlantic Ocean. It gleams with bioluminescent colour when it wants to attract a mate. Like many glowing critters, it is highly venomous.

BEARDED FIREWORM

A BRIGHT FRIGHT

The yellow-coated clusterwink has both a funny name *and* a shell. It also puts on a vibrant lightshow. When a hungry crab gets close, the clever clusterwink flashes a strobe-like green light that is bright enough to make the crab forget what it is doing and reveal itself to crab-eating predators! That's right, this snail's shine turns the hunter into the hunted.

Only the green bioluminescence that the yellow-coated clusterwink makes can pass through its shell, which works a little bit like a lampshade. Amazingly, the shell filters the green light in just the right way to make the clusterwink seem much bigger than it really is!

YELLOW-COATED CLUSTERWINK

SHEEN QUEENS

Some animals look like they're glowing, but their radiant shine comes from iridescence. This trick of the light gives some materials, such as shells or feathers, a glossy sheen similar to that found in a rainbow bubble or an oil slick.

Iridescence is often caused by diffraction, which is when waves of light bend around an object instead of being absorbed by it. You can see this when you look at a prism. Iridescence is most obvious when you change your angle of view, or when light hits in a certain direction.

SOUTHERN CASSOWARY

ULYSSES BUTTERFLY

NOT JUST FOR LOOKS

Most colours you see in animals come from pigments in their skin or hair. But tiny structures in the outer coverings of iridescent animals make them gleam in the light. You may have seen shiny fish and snake scales, but did you know butterflies are 'scaly', too? Microscopic scales on their wings overlap to create iridescence. This 'glow up' doesn't just make them pretty. Like other forms of glowing, it can help them attract mates, blend in with their surroundings, or startle predators.

The Australian water python is a real life 'rainbow serpent'. Its scales shimmer with colour in the sunlight.

WATER PYTHON

BIRDWING BUTTERFLY

FANCY FEATHERS

Many birds, including the jabiru, satin bowerbird, blue-winged kookaburra, southern cassowary, and glossy and straw-necked ibises, have microscopic structures and tiny air cavities in the keratin that makes up their feathers. These bend the light, like a prism, and gleam.

STRAW-NECKED IBIS FEATHERS

NIGHT LIGHTS

Scientists learn new things all the time. Recently, they found out that lots of animals glow under ultraviolet light, including Australian mammals such as the platypus, wombat, greater bilby and Tasmanian devil. Why these animals are **BIOFLUORESCENT** remains a mystery.

Researchers used to think that nocturnal mammals couldn't see UV light. Now that we think they *can* see it, because some of them glow too, we have even more questions! Could it be that it helps them recognise members of their own species from a distance, so they know it is safe to go closer?

TASMANIAN DEVIL

SHOULD I STAY OR SHOULD I GLOW?

Scorpions are some of the most amazing glowers on land, but they don't make their own light. They're fluorescent, only glowing when ultraviolet light shines on them. Scorpions are **NOCTURNAL** arthropods that hunt in the dark and wear their skeletons outside their bodies. A scorpion's exoskeleton senses UV light, which may help it work out how bright the moon is. When the moon is full, a scorpion may be too visible to its predators, so glowing may help them know when to stay home!

Some believe the scorpion's glow is from times when its predators were blind to UV, like humans. But many reptiles and birds (and even mammals) can see UV, and so can many invertebrates. So ... scorpio, scorpio, why do you glow?

SCORPION

BRIGHT BUGS

Some of the most famous glowers are fireflies and glow worms. But did you know that fireflies aren't true flies (they're beetles) and glow worms aren't true worms (they're baby flies, or larvae)?

Fireflies live all over the world, with more than 20 species in Australia. They make their own light from luciferin, luciferase and oxygen. They even use oxygen inside their bodies to make flashing patterns that change from species to species.

A special group of glowing insects called glow worms is only found in Australia and New Zealand. Glow worms live in caves or in shaded gullies and hang on long threads of silk covered in droplets. These sticky strings are traps for insects, just like spider webs.

IF FIREFLIES WEREN'T DISCOVERED FIRST, GLOW WORMS MAY HAVE BEEN CALLED FIREFLIES, AND FIREFLIES MIGHT HAVE BEEN CALLED BRIGHT BEETLES!

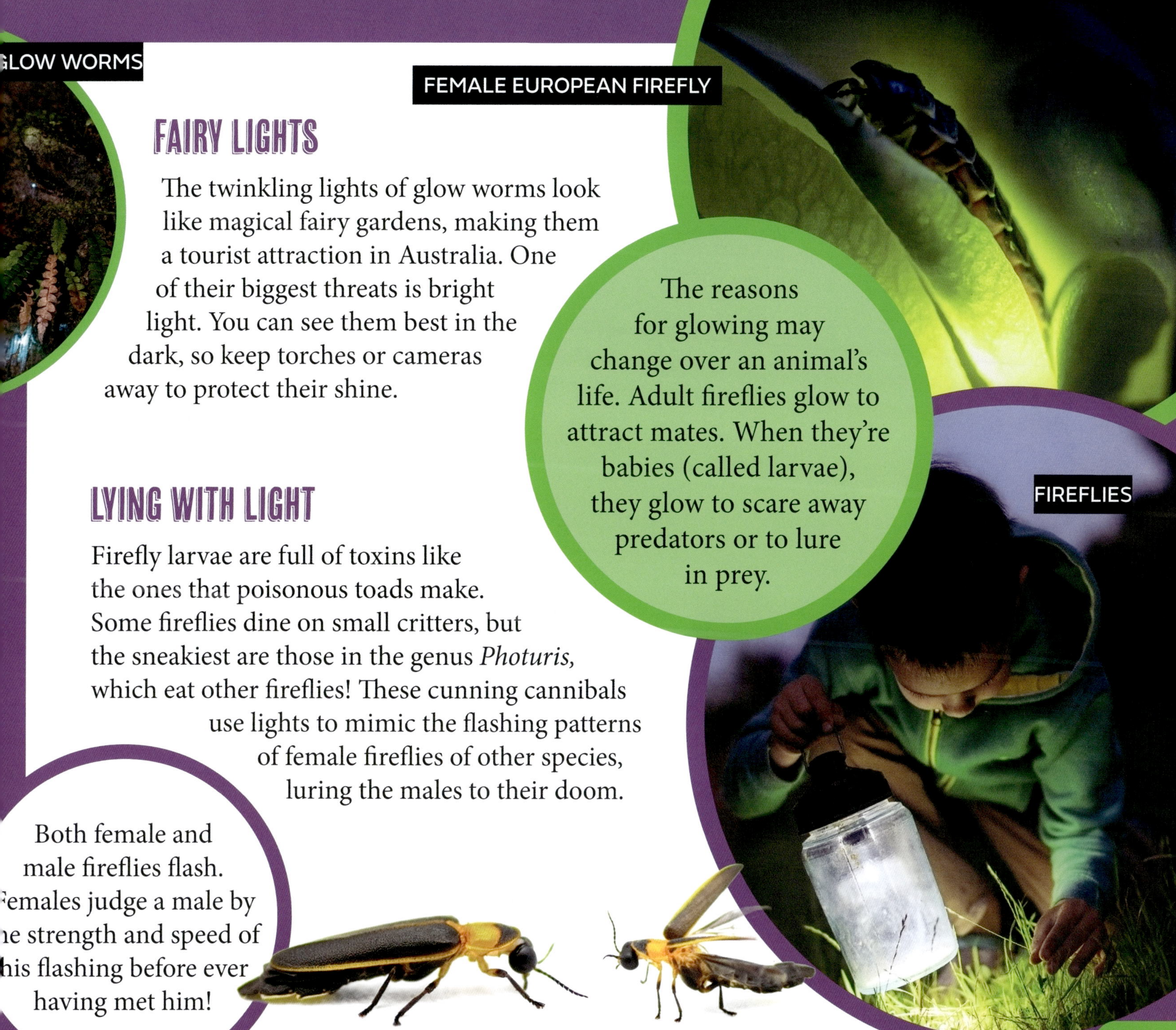

FAIRY LIGHTS

The twinkling lights of glow worms look like magical fairy gardens, making them a tourist attraction in Australia. One of their biggest threats is bright light. You can see them best in the dark, so keep torches or cameras away to protect their shine.

The reasons for glowing may change over an animal's life. Adult fireflies glow to attract mates. When they're babies (called larvae), they glow to scare away predators or to lure in prey.

LYING WITH LIGHT

Firefly larvae are full of toxins like the ones that poisonous toads make. Some fireflies dine on small critters, but the sneakiest are those in the genus *Photuris,* which eat other fireflies! These cunning cannibals use lights to mimic the flashing patterns of female fireflies of other species, luring the males to their doom.

Both female and male fireflies flash. Females judge a male by the strength and speed of his flashing before ever having met him!

WE GLOW TOGETHER

Corals are made up of colonies of tiny organisms called polyps that live in a symbiotic relationship with algae. Algae aren't plants, but they're more like plants than like animals. Like plants, these zooxanthellae algae use photosynthesis to make their own food from sunlight. Their energy helps the corals, sponges and sea jellies they live inside glow.

FLUORESCENT CORALS

FRIENDS FOR LIFE

Algae make light into food, but they need just the right amount of light to do it. If the sea gets too warm, coral and their algae friends are forced to part, and coral bleaching happens. To get dinner on the table, coral start to make large amounts of green fluorescent proteins, which protect algae from too much sunlight. It's kind of like wearing bright green zinc sunscreen. By reflecting some wavelengths of light, corals protect their tiny friends.

ELEPHANT EAR CORAL

Corals mostly grow in shallow seas that have lots of light for zooxanthellae to turn into food. In the depths, where there isn't enough light for algae, corals use red fluorescent protein to turn blue light into an orange glow that zooxanthellae can use to make nutrients. This helps corals survive if the waters get muddy. But it isn't the only reason deep-sea corals glow. In the darkness, corals can't live by light alone, so deepwater corals fluoresce to invite curious shrimp to drop by for dinner. Yum, yum!

& GROW TOGETHER

ZOANTHUS POLYPS ARE A TYPE OF CORAL

DISCO IN THE DEEP

Most of the glowing that goes on happens in the world's oceans. Whether in deep or shallow water, fish, sharks and rays, molluscs and other marine invertebrates find ways to stand out and shine under water.

SHINY SHENANIGANS

Some fish have iridescent scales or spots, including the beaked leatherjacket and the yellowtail damselfish. Others are biofluorescent under some lights, like the lumpfish, and yet others, such as the pineapplefish, have bioluminescent 'headlights' they use to scan the sea floor for food.

YELLOWTAIL DAMSELFISH

BEAKED LEATHERJACKET

PINEAPPLEFISH

LUMPFISH

TRICK OF THE LIGHT

The coconut octopus lives in the Pacific and Indian Oceans. It is super smart, even collecting coconut shells to wear as armour! But it's not clever enough to make its own light.

COCONUT OCTOPUS

What looks like bioluminescence on the coconut octopus's tentacles is just high contrast between pale and dark colours. In the blue of its ocean home, it looks like it's glowing. You might notice a similar thing if you wear white clothes to a school disco.

OPHIUROIDEA

BRITTLE STAR

Some brittle stars and sea cucumbers have flashing limbs they can drop off to confuse predators and make a quick getaway!

Moon jellies have no heart or brain, but they do have true bioluminescence. Their glow is formed by symbiosis and used to attract mates or prey.

MOON JELLIES

MUSHY MAGIC

Animals aren't the only organisms that glow. More than 100 species of glowing fungi (or mushrooms) exist worldwide. Fungi may seem like plants because they don't move much, but they're more closely related to animals.

Australia is home to a glowing fungus called the ghost mushroom. It uses luciferin, luciferase and oxygen to make its incredibly bright gleam. It is fascinating that creatures such as fireflies and mushrooms somehow find the same ways to signal to other species. When the same trait or survival skill evolves in many different species, it is known as **CONVERGENT EVOLUTION**.

GHOST FUNGUS BY NIGHT

HONEY FUNGUS IN A JAR

The world's most widespread bioluminescent fungus is the honey fungus (*Armillaria mellea*) found in Europe, America, Asia and South Africa.

GREEN PEPE

SHINE BY NIGHT

More than 100 species of mushroom glow, including some *Mycena* species found in Australia, such as the green pepe. Glowing uses energy, so most mushrooms don't do it during the day. However, some species that live in rotting wood have a faint glow all the time, which is known as 'foxfire'.

MORE SPORES

Mushrooms can't move, so they have to solve the problem of how to spread their seed so their offspring don't compete with them for nutrients. Fungi 'seeds' are called spores, and the mushroom is just a small part of a much larger underground organism. By glowing at night, ghost mushrooms attract beetles, insects, and red triangle slugs, which feed on them and spread the mushroom's spores far and wide.

If a large animal, such as a human, came along and ate the ghost mushroom, the spores would be gone (and the person may get very sick), so the ghost mushroom's glow doubles as a warning that it is poisonous.

GHOST FUNGUS BY DAY

GLOWING FOR GOLD

Marine creatures and mushrooms aren't the only clever critters getting around. Humans like to create glowing things as well. We often copy the smart things other organisms have made and use them to solve our own problems.

DID YOU KNOW?

Researchers around the globe have injected fluorescent proteins from jellyfish DNA into the embryos of pigs, rabbits, fish and even wildcats to make cloned glow-in-the-dark critters! The GloFish is the first genetically modified (GM) fish to be sold as a pet in some parts of the world. GM pets are not allowed in Australia.

GLOFISH

Researchers can inject fluorescent proteins into cells to track microscopic activities that happen inside the body and to figure out which cells signal to each other and why. This has helped scientists learn a lot about how the human body works, so they can make better medicines.

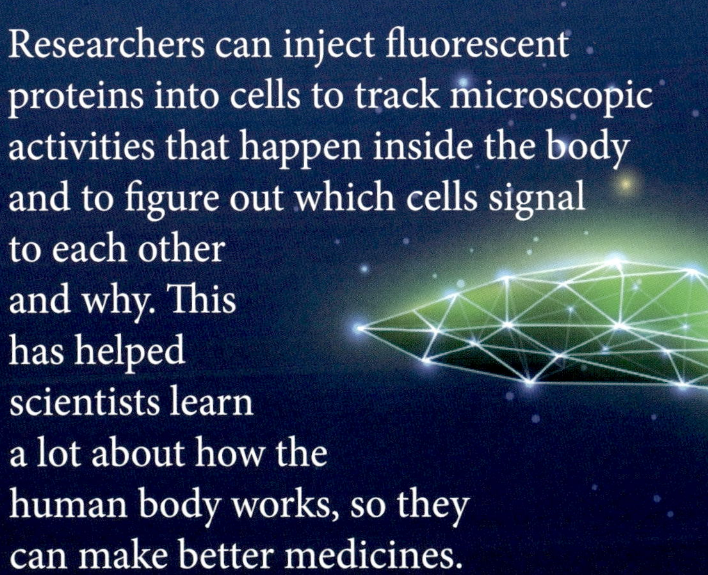

FUTURE GLOW?

Maybe one day we'll have huge bioluminescent trees that light up at night to power street lights and reduce our carbon output. Anything is possible – if you just give it a 'glow'!

Luminol is a chemical that glows when it touches blood or body fluids. Police use it to detect blood and other evidence at crime scenes.

THE POLICE USE GLOWING TECHNOLOGY TO SOLVE CRIMES

GLOSSARY

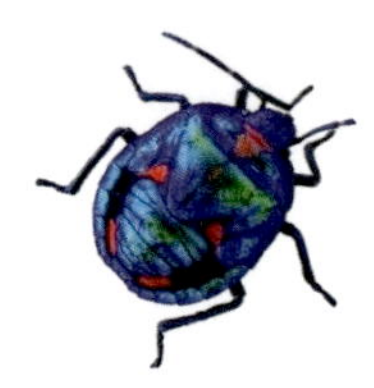

BIOFLUORESCENT
Biological things that glow under fluorescent lights.

BIOLUMINESCENT
Able to emit light as part of an organism's biology.

CONVERGENT EVOLUTION
When the same traits evolve in organisms of different types independently.

ENDOSYMBIOSIS
When organisms work together with one living inside the other.

FLUORESCENT
Glowing under some wavelengths of light.

INCANDESCENT
Emitting light that is caused by heat.

IRIDESCENT
Glowing when light waves bend around or bounce off an object.

LUCIFERASE
An enzyme found in the luminous organs of some organisms.

LUMINESCENT
Able to emit light that isn't caused by heat.

NOCTURNAL
Active by night.

PHOSPHORESCENT
Giving off light with little or no heat, sometimes due to the presence of phosphorus.

PHOTOPHORES
Light-emitting organs that some organisms have.

SYMBIOSIS
When organisms need each other to survive and therefore live and work together.

WAVELENGTH
A way of measuring waves in the time it takes for a cycle from crest to crest.

PICTURE CREDITS

Images are listed clockwise from top left unless specified.
AG = Australian Geographic; SS = Shutterstock.com;
US = Unsplash.com; CP = CanvaPro

Front cover: Eric Isselee/SS; Vojce/SS; Folgen/Pixabay; Carolyn Smith1/SS; Joe Belanger/SS; Anna-Nas/SS; Martin Valigursky/SS; Shayna Bepple/US; yod 67/SS; Gerald Robert Fischer/SS. **1:** Zuzha/SS; Shaun Jeffers/SS; 7activestudio/CP; Vojce/SS; FriedGreenTomates/CP; Daniel Garrido/Getty Images. **2:** ZetongLi/Pexels. **3:** Reklamer/SS; Trevor McKinnon/US; KevinPhillips_27707/Pixabay; SS/Vitaly Korovin. **4:** RugliG/CP; SvetaZi/SS. **5:** italianestro/SS; Purrfect_photo/SS. **6:** Alessandro Bianchi/US; Sam Robertshaw/SS; NOAA PhotoLibrary/Flickr **7:** piyaphong/SS; SuperJospephCP; NOAAPhotoLibrary_PD/Flickr; Steven Haddock/Monterey Bay Aquarium Research Institute. **8:** Souvik Sarkar Photography/SS. **9:** Vadim Sadovski/SS; Will Turner/US. **10:** Maxfield Weakley/SS; Roy Caldwell/UC Berkeley; Roy Caldwell/UC Berkeley. **11:** Richard Whitcombe/SS; DiveIvanov/SS; Langdon Quetin and Robin Ross, Marine Science Institute, University of California, Santa Barbara; Martin Prochazkacz/SS. **12:** David A Litman/SS. RobJ808/SS. **13:** Tracey Winholt/SS; Neil Bromhall/SS. **14:** Sylke Rohrlach/Wikimedia Commons; Xanth Haung/Flickr. **15:** Dr Dimitri Deheyn, Scripps Oceanography, UC San Diego; Gerald Robert Fischer/SS. **16:** AlexanderLesnitsky/Pixabay; Carolyn Smith1/SS; YAKOBCHUK V/SS; 17234435/Pixabay; Here/SS. **17:** Martin Valigursky (top right)/SS; Ondrej Prosicky/SS; Georgina Steytler/AG (bottom left). **18:** Gokhan Dogan/SS; Peter Francis/SS; Gapvoy/SS. **19:** Netscape/SS; Leon Pauleikhoff/US. **20:** Martin Vinas (background)/Dreamstime; Martin Prochazkacz/SS; Grant Sloane/SS. **21:** Wirestock Creators/SS; EvgeniiAnd/SS; Chase D'animulls/SS. **22:** David Clode/US; Zurijeta/US. **23:** Jen Watson/SS; Vojce/SS. **24:** Cingular/SS; Joe Belanger/SS; Maxim Khytra/SS; Podolnaya Elena/SS. **25:** Saulich Elena/SS; Cingular/SSS; Furzyk73/Dreamstime; Waraporn Chokchaiworarat/SS. **26:** Petar B Photography/SS; Mindaugas Gaspa dangdumrong/SS. **27:** bonchan/SS; Anne Hayes/AG. **28:** Mediashop Productions LLC (background)/SS; Souvik Sarkar Photography/SS; Valentin Kundeus/SS. 29: Butusova Elena/SS; Couperfield/SS. **30:** Shayna Bepple/US; Tibor Molnar/SS;.**31:** James Lee/US.
Back cover: David Clode/US.

Australian Geographic

DISCOVER

Australian Geographic *Discover: Glowing Animals* is published by Australian Geographic.

First published in 2023

52–54 Turner St, Redfern, NSW

editorial@ausgeo.com.au
australiangeographic.com.au

ISBN: 978-1-922388-93-3

Author: Dr Timothy N. W. Jackson
Commissioning Editor: Karin Cox
Creative Director: Aleksandra Beare
Designer: Paul Hodge
Editor: Michele Perry
Print production: Andy Franks

AUSTRALIAN GEOGRAPHIC
Managing Director: David Haslingden
Director of Content: Liz Ginis
Licensing and Publishing Manager: Tom Bates
Commercial Assistant: Felicity McManus

Printed in China by C & C Offset Printing Co. Ltd.
The paper in this book is FSC® certified. FSC® promotes environmentally responsible, socially beneficial and economically viable management of the world's forests.

BOOKS IN THIS SERIES

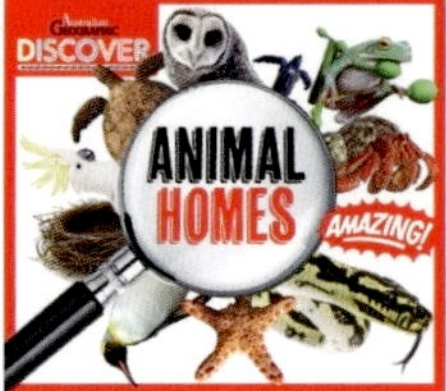

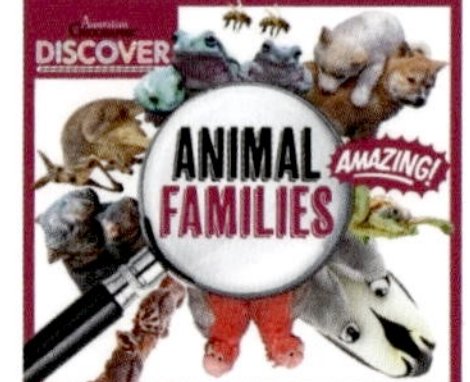

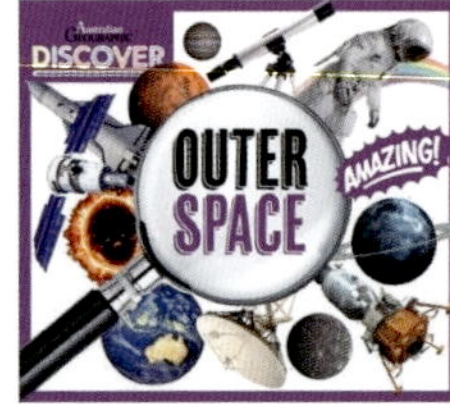

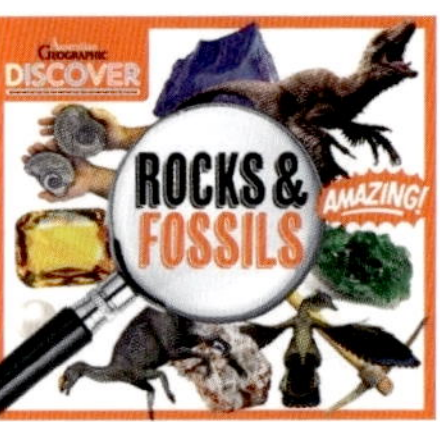

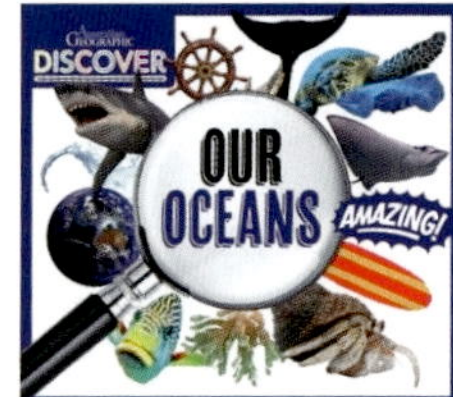

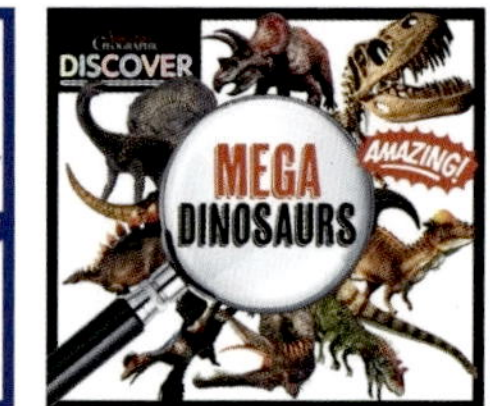

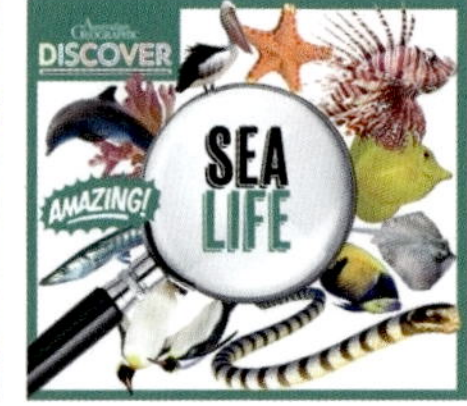

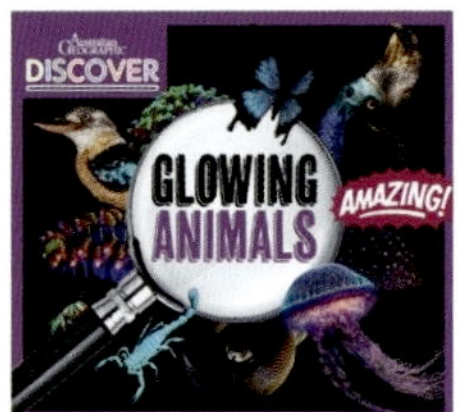

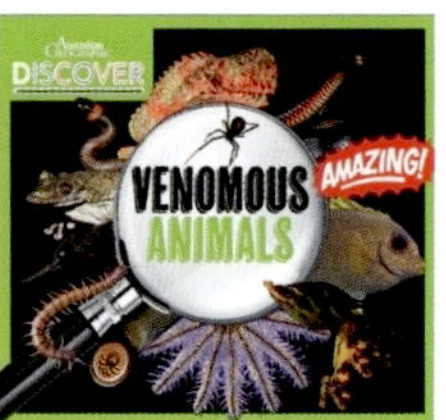

Australian Geographic contributes 100% of its profits to the Australian Geographic Society, including its conservation and sustainability programs.